Charles Brockden Brown

A Study of Early American Fiction

BY

MARTIN S. VILAS, A. M.

FOLCROFT LIBRARY EDITIONS / 1973

Library of Congress Cataloging in Publication Data

Vilas, Martin Samuel.
  Charles Brockden Brown.

  1. Brown, Charles Brockden, 1771-1810.
PS1137.V5 1973   813'.2   73-1179
ISBN 0-8414-2750-X

Charles Brockden Brown

A Study of Early American Fiction

BY

MARTIN S. VILAS, A. M.

BURLINGTON, VT.

FREE PRESS ASSOCIATION,

1904.

The interest in Charles Brockden Brown and his works arises largely from his ranking position among American Prose Writers. Hence, it is not expected that an estimate, somewhat extended and somewhat critical, of his writings is likely to become popular. No other than this, save very brief sketches of Brown and of what he has done, is known to the writer. It may be, then, that the student of American literature will find in this book, written five years ago, something suggestive, perhaps something usually called original.

MARTIN S. VILAS.

1904.

CONTENTS

CHAPTER I.

CHAPTER II.

CHAPTER III.

CHAPTER IV.

CHARLES BROCKDEN BROWN.

A Study of Early American Fiction.

CHAPTER I.

CONDITION OF LITERATURE WHEN BROWN WROTE.

Literatures like Constitutions are not made; they grow. Like the growth of the coal mine, they form, harden and mature from the timber of other ages, of times well nigh forgotten, and from materials usually overlooked by the ninety and nine. Literature is the clear lake in which may be seen mirrored the vegetation that grows near it, the animal life that appears above and around it and the movements within its horizon.

That the beginnings of every nation in literature have been in verse, not prose; that the development of her prose has seldom antedated the development of her material resources is something generally recognized as almost a truism in the history of literatures. In the United States we note the rare exception. The rule has been true because with most nations we mark their rise from a condition of barbarism by long, slow stages to civilization and culture. The people in the early periods of progression have not the intellects capable of carrying on the successive steps in argumentative prose but their fancies are pleased by ballads descriptive of the heroism of themselves and their ancestors. But America received her origin and early development not through an Anchises and an Aeneas carrying their *"sacra patriosque penates"* to found a new city to rise by the fostering care of Olympus, nor yet, through a Hengist and a Horsa that bore to new shores a barbarous vigor and independence, but she received them at a stage in the world's history when the blackness of ten centuries of gloom had but fairly rolled away, when the civilized world, rejoicing anew in its rediscovered strength, was investigating and progressing as never before and had sent some of its best blood across the western seas to colonize and found new nations. The long years of evolution from the uncivilized to the civilized that marked the growth of European nations were absent here. For without the institutions of the Old World, the New yet possessed their training and influence and considered herself as good as her fathers. The United States, though her tuition has been derived from all the world, yet is in language, institutions and laws, the child of England. To her she has ever turned to draw the inspiration that has set her alive to the best instincts within herself.

Moreover, poetry, the language of passion and imagination, could have, at the beginning not much in common with our fore-fathers unless it be used to illustrate some teaching of their strict Calvanism or to warn more effectively than could prose the sinner heedless of the coming "Day of Doom." To subdue the forests, to clear the land, till the fields and build homes amid an environment of savage beasts and savage men required a strong arm and a stout heart with but little demand

for the intellectual training that was able to present the
best of the new renaissance which was moving Europe
from the Mediterranean to the Arctic Ocean.

When to the stern realities of their natural surroundings, were added the yet sterner ones of political
oppression from the mother country, we find a condition
which exercised the minds of America along lines averse
to scholarly ease and enjoyment but which caused the
latent culture of their intellects to spring up in vigorous
oratorical and argumentative prose,—that form of literature which, first after the distinctively religious, finds
place in our literary history. Until the new nation was
established on an independent basis there were but few
opportunities for the fostering of even that kind of literature best suited to the tastes of Americans, save as the
necessities of the times called it into play and gave it
tone and finish. Her Mathers and her Edwards had no
use for stories to entertain. Their time was occupied
with the saving of souls while the spirit which Macaulay[1]
says was employed to suppress bear-baiting—"not because it gave pain to the bear, but because it gave
fun to the audience"—was exercised also against fiction.
Her men of scholarly tastes, her Otis and her Hamilton,
must look to the great interests of the nation regardless
of the delights of pure literature.

After 1789 it took a number of years for the nation
to find herself, to realize that she was a nation and that
others expected of her in all respects a nation's work.
To England we still turned our eyes in all things, and

1 Macaulay's Hist. 1, Ch. 2.

as a nation that had gained its independence by force from her and one that was still treated with ill-disguised contempt by Great Britain, the United States felt much emulation to try its pinions on flights attempted with such wonderful success by the long line of English men of letters. In the words of Prof. Beers,[1] "An effort was made to establish by *tour de force,* a national literature of a bigness commensurate with the scale of American nature and of the destinies of the new republic." Even the gallant deeds of the revolution remained unsung. To quote from Stedman[2], "No poetry was begotten in the rage of that heroic strife; its humor, hatred, hope, suffering, prophecy, were feebly uttered so far as verse were concerned, in the mode and language inherited years before from the coarsest English satirists. Some few original notes were heard among our pipings."[2]

But in prose dressed in the garb of peace when the great need for Henry and Adams had died away, America's record was bare of excellencies and even the mother country had only an inartistic beginning to its credit. The "Ten linked chain" of the artificial school of Pope had for a century and a half bound English verse. It was necessary to go back to Pope and Goldsmith or take up with Darwin and Hayley. The new natural school, at the head of which were Thomson, Gray, Cowper and Burns, had not then gained much influence, while Wordsworth, Coleridge and Southey were too ardently democratic to gain at once great strength on this side of the Atlantic. Scott, Byron, Keats, Shelley and

1. Beers.   2. Stedman. Poets of Am. p. 16.

Tennyson were yet to come. The new life from Carlyle
and Macaulay had not at that time been infused into
history and essay. The various phases of social life had
not been held up to view by Dickens and Thackeray and
the Edinburgh *Review*, which afterward exercised so
wide an influence through Brougham, Sidney Smith and
Jeffrey, was yet to enter upon its career.

Not till the eighteenth century was well started,
had prose fiction been cultivated by English authors.
Sidney's Arcadia, Bacon's Atlantis and More's Utopia
hardly entitled them to a place in the literature of fiction; so that Daniel De Foe is said to be the founder
of the English novel. After him, the names of Richardson, Fielding, Smollett and Sterne appeared with greatest prominence. Near the close of the century the novel
as written by Fielding gave way to the romance and
Mrs. Ann Radcliffe became the most popular English
writer of fiction. Her greatest works, "The Romance
of the Forest," and "The Mysteries of Udolpho," attracted considerable attention. At about the same time
came Horace Walpole's "The Castle of Otranto," William Beckford's "Vathek," M. G. Louis's "The Monk,"
and "Tales of Terror," Mrs. Shelley's "Frankestein,"
William Godwin's "Caleb Williams" and Jane Austen's
"Pride and Prejudice." But Jane Austen hardly be-
longs to the same class with those preceding her in
the list. The tone of her writings is more healthful and
in style she has more connection to the later school of
Scott than to the morbid spirit of these "Pestilent Night-
s."

In the United States it might seem that the scenes
of the Colonial and Revolutionary Wars formed the
most fitting setting for romance, but the perspective of
romance needs to be at some distance from the present
to be able to gather to itself the glamour of imaginative
glory. I quote from Prescott[1] : "Great doubts were long
entertained for our capabilities for immediate success in
this department. We had none of the buoyant, stirring
associations of a romantic age; none of the chivalrous
pageantry, the feudal and border story or Robin Hood
Adventure; none of the dim shadowy superstitions and
the traditional legends which had gathered like moss
round every stone, hill and valley of the olden country.
Everything here wore a spick-and-span new aspect and
lay in the broad, garish sunshine of every day life. We
had none of the picturesque varieties of situation or cos-
tume; everything lay on the same dull, prosaic level, in
short, we had none of the most obvious elements of
poetry; at least so it appeared to the vulgar eye."[1] In
the last decade of the eighteenth century Mrs. Rowson
sent forth "Charlotte Temple, A Tale of Truth." In
the words of Richardson,[2] "Its long drawn melancholy
is unrelieved by a touch of art; it is not even amusing
in its absurdity." Soon after came "Female Quixotism"
by Mrs. Tenney, which is aptly described by the above
characterization of "Charlotte Temple." American men
of culture felt that they must do something to show
their independence of England and their equality of in-

1. Prescott's Miscellanies, C. B. Brown, p. 51.
2. Richardson A. Lit., Vol. 11, p. 285.

tellect and training. Dwight and Freneau had exhibited this spirit in the realm of poetry but in the domain of prose fiction, save for the lachrymose productions of Mrs. Rowson and Mrs. Tenney, nothing deserved the name. Even Hawthorne in his preface to "The Marble Faun" complains of his position in words that more fitly apply to the time of which we speak. "No author without a trial, can conceive of the difficulty of writing a romance about a country where there is no shadow, no antiquity, no mystery, no picturesque and gloomy wrong, nor anything but a common-place prosperity in broad and simple daylight as is happily the case with my dear, native land. It will be very long, I trust, before romance writers may find congenial and easily handled themes, either in the annals of our stalwart republic, or in any characteristic and probable events of our individual lives. Romance and poetry, ivy, lichens, and wall-flowers need ruin to make them grow."

CHAPTER II.

CHARLES BROCKDEN BROWN.

Probably no author could have felt more this dearth of suitable surroundings than Charles Brockden Brown, who stands to American fiction as Daniel De Foe to the English novel. Born in Philadelphia of Quaker ancestry January 17, 1771, his naturally delicate constitution was rendered still more fragile by his retiring, sedentary habits. From early childhood he was an earnest student and an omnivorous reader, possessing one of those minds that by intuition grasp and absorb all things "bookish" within reach of it. At the age of 16, he had planned three epic poems on the discovery of America and the conquests of Peru and Mexico. Fortunately for him, no vestige of these now remains. Not long after, he began the study of law but soon abandoned that profession, for which he was unfitted, and gave himself entirely to literature or "bookmaking"[1] as he called it.

In 1798 he may be said to have made his permanent home in New York City, after frequent visits and here he published his first romance, "Wieland," four years after the publication of William Godwin's "Caleb Williams." The second novel of Brown, "Ormond," appeared in 1799. These two works excited much interest on both sides of the Atlantic and considerable favorable comment arose from literary men upon the unusual

1. Duyckinck's Cyclo. of Am. Lit., Vol. 1, p. 612.

powers of conception and execution displayed in them. This was undoubtedly pleasing to Brown, as it would be to anyone, and served to reconcile him more fully to his unique position in the United States. In 1798 the yellow fever visited New York City with a violence similar to that which had marked its appearance in Philadelphia five years before. On account of the presence of his friend, Dr. E. H. Smith, a young man of much promise, in the city, Brown refused to leave New York. Soon after the death of Dr. Smith from the disease, Brown was himself taken down with it and nearly died. Upon his recovery he gave forth his third romance, "Arthur Mervyn; or Memoirs of the Year 1793," a story laid near Philadelphia, which gives a supposed account of the yellow fever as it came upon that city. This was succeeded soon after by "Edgar Huntly; or The Adventures of a Sleep-walker," a wild imaginative tale. Brown published "Clara Howard" in 1801 and in 1804 appeared "Jane Talbot," first published in England, the last of the six works of fiction that form the basis of Brown's reputation and of what I shall say of his works.

Only little more need be said of Brown save in direct reference to these six. During the year he published "Clara Howard," he returned to his native city and made his home in the family of his brother. Here in 1803 he undertook the management of "Literary Magazine and American Register." Brown had in 1799 established the "Monthly Magazine and American Review" in New York City, which did not survive the year, but the "Register" maintained a life of considerable vigor for five years. During the last years of his life, Brown wrote several political pamphlets, which detracted nothing from his reputation and a number of biographical works were added to his name. The health of the author, always delicate and infirm, now began to give way entirely under what appeared to be consumption and he died on the 22d of February, 1810, aged 39, leaving a wife and four children.

In the prose fiction of Brown there is to me much more of the romance than of the novel,—though it would seem that in most he intended to make them a recital of the events of real life and not to place in them so much of the lofty and supernatural as to entitle them to the designation of romances; but it was difficult for Brown to write what we to-day consider a novel. His mind was too morbid, too much absorbed with that which is beyond it all.

CHAPTER III.

WIELAND.

In none of our author's romances is the ruling spirit of his mind shown out with so great distinctness as in his first, "Wieland, or the Transformation," which is commonly said to be similar to Godwin's "Caleb Williams." Indeed, the influence of Godwin is apparently clear, but it seems to me impossible for Brown to write similarly to another. Both stories start with an idea which is to be worked out according to the theory of the author and events as we go on shape themselves to a form suitable for this. Godwin wrote his story to show forth the evils of the social system in England, how utterly impossible it was for the poor to contend for justice against the rich or noble and to illustrate how the remnants of the spirit of chivalry in England might affect a mind morbidly sensitive to the dictates of "honor." In "Wieland" we have the ill effects that might arise from the use of ventriloquism and a demonstration of the advisability of keeping one's mind clear of fanciful theories. In both there is a conception of a grim destiny that pursues and overhangs its object as relentlessly as the night follows the day. The victims of this destiny have forebodings of impending doom and are gloomy. They writhe and struggle, but there is no escape. Nevertheless, the mind of Brockden Brown was peculiar unto himself and that peculiarity leaves its impress on everything that he wrote.

The scene of "Wieland" is laid in Pennsylvania among a family named Wieland of German descent, cultivated and of excellent standing. The contemplation of religious topics seems inherited. The father has died in a mysterious and terrible manner and the son has derived from him a melancholy and superstitious constitution of mind, which his studious habits and uneventful life have developed into an amiable fanaticism. The family live close to the Schuykill; near by is the sister who tells the story and the most of the time Pleyel, the brother of Wieland's wife. Strange voices are heard by different members of the family, sometimes commanding them to do certain acts, warning them of danger or telling them of events beyond the reach of human knowledge. The "dead vast and middle of the night" is employed for these things, which affect the head of the family in particular as indications of a supernatural agency. A destiny of horror seems to hang over the family and we read on anticipating some dread event.

About this time a middle aged man named Carwin of rustic appearance, comes to them somewhat mysteriously. In spite of his apparent rusticity, his knowledge and readiness are unlimited and invariable. There is wonderful music in his voice which affects the sister particularly in a most powerful manner. The attractiveness of his conversation is such that he is admitted to great intimacy at Mettingen, the home of Wieland. The strange voices and warnings of danger increase in frequency, the perplexity and apprehension of the family are daily augmented and all seem to wait anxiously for the denouement. At length on the bidding of a solemn, mysterious voice, Wieland offers up on the alter of a submissive piety his wife and young children and attempts the life of his sister who escapes by accident. He is arrested, convicted of murder, and confined in a dungeon as a lunatic, but bears it all with the heroic calmness of one confident that he has fulfilled the will of the Almighty. During an escape, he learns that he has been deceived and misguided by the ventriloquism of Carwin, who, prompted by pure malice, has taken pleasure in playing his tricks upon the family. The wretched Wieland, in the frenzy of the discovery, kills himself and the now regretful Carwin disappears from the scene and the story closes with the marriage of the sister and Pleyel, whose bride has recently died. | As the moral of the story, so far as the family is concerned, the author, supposedly the sister, states "If Wieland had framed juster notions of moral duty and of the divine attributes, or if I had been gifted with ordinary equanimity or foresight, the double-tongued deceiver would have been baffled and repelled."[1]

Griswold in his "Prose Writers of America,"[2] takes issue with the author in calling Carwin a "demon," "fiend" and actuated by "diabolical malice," but much allowance must be made for the horror of those represented as present at the time. Certainly, it is difficult to see how one could take a pleasure in doing what the ventriloquist did here without it is a "fiendish" and "devilish" pleasure and actuated by " diabolical malice."

1. "Wieland," p. 251.
2. P. 108.

The method of explaining the death of the elder
Wieland by spontaneous combustion was one that Brown
obtained from the doctors as he indicates in a foot note.[1]
It was a favorite device of the author to introduce something that had especially attracted his interest into his
works, then give a reference to explain it in a foot note,
as in this instance and that of ventriloquism.[2]

Griswold[3] can see nothing peculiar in people of the
education and intellect of this family being thus de-
ceived, nor does he think that the explanation given of
these mysteries "renders it in any degree uninteresting,"
but Prof. Beers refers to the ventriloquism of
"Wieland" under the statement that "Brown frequently
raises a superstructure of mystery on a basis ludicrously
weak." Such cases certainly have been known, but the
training of the people must have been unusual to admit
of it, and I do not agree with Griswold[5] that Brown was
"a careful anatomist of the mind and familiar with its
wonderful phenomena." It is true that he evidently had
made a careful study of the mind, but that he ever un-
derstood its healthy workings I do not believe. To do
this one must himself possess a mind that has for considerable periods of time felt the delight of living in that
state of semi-unconsciousness to our physical being which
we call health. So only will he be able to feel as other

1. "Wieland," p. 38.
2. "Wieland," p. 207.
3. Prose Writers of Am., p. 109.
4. Am. Lit., p. 82.
5. Prose Writers of Am., p. 109.

men have felt and usually feel, to come in contact with and measure himself by the common standard. This great pleasure and power we are assured Brown never possessed; accordingly, he was given constantly to introspection and self-contemplation. If the chimeras and superstitious vagaries of "Wieland" obtained credence in a family of education and strength of mind to-day, we should consider them fit inmates for an insane asylum; certainly, for a retreat for nervous invalids. No man of good intelligence simply because he hears a mysterious voice destroys his loved ones unless crazy or a religious fanatic.

As to the lack of strength in the explanation, it does not seem to me to be a source of strength. To make it successful, the primary cause must be assigned to glaring mental weakness; then when we are wrought up by the horrors and pathos of the story, it turns out to be the miserable trick of a miserable adventurer. And the involuntary feeling is to wish much that we had been present to inflict summary punishment on the malicious wretch and tell Wieland, "man of sorrows" though he be, what a miserable, wretched idiot and hideous criminal he has been. The transition is too sudden.

The pathos and horror of the preceding scenes are worthy of a sterner setting. In Wieland's description of the destruction of his wife, so dear to him, there is an intensity of the terrible equal to some of the best passages of the kind in any language known to me. All the ghastliness of Euripides' Medea or of Lady Macbeth walking in her sleep while she rubs her hands and ejaculates "Here's the smell of blood still! All the perfumes of Arabia will not sweeten this little hand! Oh! Oh! Oh!"[1] gives not so much horror to the surroundings as does Brown here while there is an added pathetic element that appeals to our tenderest sympathies.

But, if Brown introduced the mystery at all, he must needs explain it in some such way. Our education is too advanced and our ideas too open to admit of other expedients save those of the juggler. It is this that makes the trick beyond success to the healthy mind under any circumstances. We have no atmosphere of superstition which will allow it. Scott in his treatment of the Scottish Highlands had a location imbued with the superstitious and a people by instinct and training adapted to it. He might introduce a touch of such here and there, yet leave it unexplained. Shakespeare in Macbeth need not, for the same reason, explain the witches or Banquo's ghost; but in America in the nineteenth century nothing approaching it would go unchallenged.

But in addition to this, when we have finished "Wieland" there seems something "uncanny" about it and we cannot make ourselves believe that ordinary mortals would so conduct themselves. It is right here that I add emphasis to my criticism that Brown did not understand the human mind. If he understands it, he must be able to show forth its workings as they are so that they seem to us possible. A romance does not necessarily deal entirely with the possible, but if, in a romance, a family of our country and of recent time are taken as a basis of

1. "Macbeth."

the events, they should not act as though they belong more properly to another world than this.

Again, none of the characters are really strong characters. They are decidedly unpractical and we learn nothing from looking upon them. Great pains are taken to teach a moral, but it is a moral for the most part taught from those that are not "of the earth earthy." It was, indeed, a fault of the time that merely showed, perhaps, that Brown read the literature of the day; nevertheless, we are forced to criticise by what seems to be a common-sense standard. Of the practical, alert man or woman of affairs, there is nowhere a glimpse. The imputed authoress and heroine lives in a house by herself with a single servant and an endeavor is made to create a model womanly character of a stronger mold than the ordinary, but unexplained apprehensions constantly bring her down into the "Slough of Despond." She hears for the first time the voice of the unknown Carwin and immediately is "like Niobe, all tears," and spends the next day in musing and in gazing at her sketches of the supposed countryman. We are continually wishing that the characters had something to do, that they had less time for "musing," for "contemplation" of "thoughts ominous and dreary." We wish they would do something as we would do, were we in their places, but this they never attempt, even though their lives depend upon it.

A peculiar and exceedingly weak deviation is made at the close when we are looking with great interest to the climax by side-tracking the reader into the midst of many details in regard to "Louisa Conway, Major

Stuart, and Maxwell,"—none of whom really had anything to do with the inception and development of the plot and about none of whom do we care anything. It would seem that Brown felt bound to get another moral lesson into the work and so fastens it on at the close, since he could see no place where it was admissible.

On the other hand, there is much of strength in the romance, much to give with justice a reputation to the author. We are interested always and sometimes, yes often, in spite of ourselves. We never want to stop until we have seen the end and the ability of a strong and imaginative perception is everywhere visible; in fact, this is the most commendable quality of the whole. Since the defects of the tale are for the most part of the same general nature as the defects of contemporaneous literature, they are far more excusable. The work is one of the best of Brown's and, unquestionably, the best of its kind yet from an American.

CHAPTER IV.

QRMOND.

Ormond, the second romance of the author, is, in my judgment, his best work. The scene is placed in New York and Philadelphia and included in point of time the yellow fever period of Philadelphia. An artist of considerable skill is obliged to engage in his father's occupation of pharmacy to support his family. A young partner, seemingly indebted to him as much as possible, robs his patron and leaves him to blindness and beggary. His daughter, Constantia Dudley, an only child and the heroine of the whole, bears up most courageously with an "affection that hopes, and endures, and is patient" through trials that would have crushed a St. Simeon Stylites. The deadly work of the yellow fever gives ghastliness to the scenes through which she and her father pass. Just as the life for them seems to be a brighter one in propect, when Constantia discovers and causes to aid her, the villain that had cheated her father and the scourge of yellow fever has passed, Ormond appears upon the scene, somewhat like the dark and mysterious Carwin, with many things unknown about him, though he strives to appear all frankness.

His peculiar notions of marriage cause the death of the woman he has seemed to love until he meets Constantia. The continued friendship of Constantia for him after his base desertion of this woman, Helena Cleves,

and her consequent suicide, is one of the incongruities
of the story. The father of Constantia is murdered by
an unknown assassin and Ormond pursues the maiden
with dark forebodings as to the future. Her financial
condition bettered by the bequests of Helena, she is
about to set sail for Europe with her friend, the relator
of the trials and virtues of Constantia, when the violence of Ormond brings him to his death by the hand of
the maiden but not before he has slain in a fit of caprice
Craig, the despoiler of the fortunes of the family, who is
revealed as the assassin of Dudley at the instigation of
Ormond. The tale ends with Constantia in quiet happiness living like a vestal virgin with her friend in Europe.

The romance, on the whole, stands considerably
above others of Brown, though destitute of the power of
"Wieland." The author evidently wishes to exhibit in
Constantia a model of womanly virtue, a Lucretia without her peculiar misfortunes, one that can rise above
disappointments and adversity, the patient Evangeline,
but with a wisdom and thrift that could provide means
where none existed, retaining all the time an "idyllic
grace" and beauty. Brown's vivid impressions of the
yellow fever will not allow him to pass over the oppor-
tunity to exhibit the horrors of its ravages. He delighted to have a touch of mystery in his tales—hence
Ormond and his secret closet. Prof. Beers[1] suggests
that Ormond was an attempted reproduction of Aaron
Burr. It is not improbable. The ground of resemblance

1. American Lit., p. 81.

is broad. In the portrayal of this character, I detect
more art than anywhere else in Brown's works. The
character seems to be at all times true to the conception of him at the outset and he forms the most
brilliant production from this point of view in the work,
or, indeed, in any work of the author.

The story is, perhaps, too protracted in the part
that deals with the misfortunes of Constantia to be interesting. It is, however, difficult to paint such a character as this and reveal by many details the very "Sab-
baths of her soul" without running extreme danger of
wearying the reader and making the whole seem common-place. But Brown has done this part well, yet when
in contact with Ormond we are at times fearful that her
character will break down. When we would expect her
to deny her society to him after she has learned what
he really is, she continues the friendship to her own
evident misfortune. Notwithstanding, her personality is
a good one and her individuality strongly drawn.

The introduction of the authoress, the friend of
Constantia, to such prominence in the last part is a de-
cided weakness. There is, moreover, considerable of the
namby-pamby in making her leave her bridegroom of
a few weeks, the "silent partner," in Europe, while she
goes on a quest of many months for her lost friend.
The searcher has not seen her friend for over three
years, but is absorbed entirely in the search, now driven
into the depths of despair by the report of her death,
now borne upward into the seventh heaven of happiness
by an unexpected discovery of her alive and well, while

the solitary husband "unwept, unhonored and unsung," holds his own as best he can in far away London. This circumstance is an added argument in favor of what has already been said that Brown did not understand the workings of the human mind.

In opposition, the very positive excellence is possessed by the work, both positive and unusual for the time, of being in nearly all its bearings something entirely within the limits of a common-sense form of life. When we are able to feel that men as we find them would' have done thus in a similar position, we are pleased and interested. Writers able to create such characters endure. In the words of Irving,[1] "They have rooted themselves in the unchanging principles of human nature." Also, the style of English is less labored and stilted than in "Wieland." As a production from anyone, it was entitled to much commendation. As a production from an American, it deserved warm praise.

1. Mutability of Lit.

CHAPTER V.

ARTHUR MERVYN.

With the terrors of the plague in Philadelphia in 1793 as a surrounding, came forth Brown's next publication, "Arthur Mervyn," the principal actor of which is a country boy of delicate physique and sensitive nature. His father, a farmer with but little education, had married an ignorant servant girl of his. This drove the young man from home and he came to Philadelphia with almost no money and without friends or acquaintances. He was found one night sick with the prevailing illness near the dwelling of a physician who took him into his home and with his wife nursed him through the disease. On his recovery, he detailed his story to his benefactor and this recital forms the major part of the tale. On his arrival in the town after passing through several very strange experiences, he is engaged as secretary by Waldeck, an unscrupulous man of the world, the keeper of a fine establishment and by his means the rustic youth soon acquires many of the graces of culture. There is but little actual outline to the plot, but whatever interest is awakened, as we read, is centered around the criminal career of Waldeck, the connection of the youthful Mervyn with him and the descriptions of the yellow fever. A wonderful number of characters are brought in and the centrifugal force is in constant danger of overcoming the centripetal. Waldeck finally dies in a

debtor's prison and Mervyn marries Mrs. Fielding, a
widow of foreign birth, several years older than himself,
who, until the last part of the story, had not appeared.

The character of Mervyn is hardly a success unless
he be denominated "the boy wonder," but, though at
times of remarkable discernment of mind, he at others
acts with strange lack of foresight. Like the principal
characters in all Brown's romances, save possibly
"Ormond," he is unable to think of more than one thing
at a time, as instanced in his conduct in making the
journey on horseback with Eliza Hadwin.[1] One point
or phase of a matter gains his attention and he follows
that oblivious of all things else. It is difficult to see
how anyone of sound intelligence could act as he did
when he detailed his affection for Eliza Hadwin to Mrs.
Fielding and at the same time assured her that the one
he marries must be her "exact counterpart;"[2] yet he is
in blissful ignorance of the trend of his remarks or the
cause of the confusion awakened and when later the
kind friend, after much explanation, makes the situation plain to him he nearly faints in surprise and unexpected rapture.

Waldeck is the best drawn character but weak-
nesses in him are apparent. The general cast of his
character is that of the specious, ruthless villain and he
seems to be plotting rascality constantly, while frequently pretending contrition. Yet the author would several
times attempt to make him appear not really a villain

1. "Arthur Mervyn," Vol. II, p. 67.
2. Vol. II, p. 177.

but led on by a spirit of evil that frequently possessed
him. No one but a deep, determined villain could accom-
plish the dark deeds of Waldeck. Compunction and contrition at the murder of Watson should properly be exul-
tation, while such men as he do not leap into a river with
a sincere desire to drown themselves. We finally are
left in doubt as to whether Colvill and Waldeck are
really one or not. The melancholy close of Waldeck's
career is made a means to illustrate the social evils aris-
ing from imprisonment for debt and to show the horrors of the prison. The character of Mrs. Fielding, apparently intended to be the heroine of the story, is not
one that adds strength to the whole.

The writer expended all the art in the tale on the first
volume and the second consists in a mere multiplicity of
characters, sudden transitions and attempted dramatic
poses. The work will be read, if read at all, principally
for its excellent descriptions of the ravages of yellow
fever, which we presume to be drawn from the actual
experiences of the author. Here there is considerable
descriptive art shown and in several places an extremity
of the horrible is indicated by giving a few ghastly in-
cidentals, as in Chap. IV, Vol. 1. Had Brown cut out
one-half the story by lopping off details and extraneous
characters, the result would have been a positive improvement.

CHAPTER VI.

EDGAR HUNTLY.

"Edgar Huntly or Memoirs of a Somnambulist," followed "Arthur Mervyn." The seat of the story is in Pennsylvania near the forks of the Delaware. A friend of Huntly, named Waldegrave, suddenly disappeared and no trace of him is discovered, though the search is made far and wide and the supposition is that he has been murdered. On a return home by night, Huntly wanders along an unfrequented path and, by the light of the moon near the residence of a friend, perceives an unknown man digging in the ground under a tree and making frequent stops when he seems overcome with intense grief; soon the man closes the hole and Huntly follows him a long distance through the wood till he disappears in a cavern. The digger proves to be a sleepwalker, named Clithero, a mysterious foreigner employed in the neighborhood. The suspicion arises that Clithero is the assassin of Waldegrave and Huntly takes it upon himself to watch and follow him when sleepwalking. In carrying out his self-imposed mission, the young man meets strange adventures in the wild forest. Finally, brooding over the matter, Huntly himself walks in his sleep and on recovering his senses finds himself in a deep cavern miles from home with a panther and a small band of sleeping Indians between himself and the open air. He slays the panther and one of the Indians

and effects his escape, taking with him a prisoner of the
Indians, a young girl whom he rescued. In completing
their escape, Huntly meets a number of encounters with
the Indians and behaves with considerable bravery and
resolution. After passing through great hardships and
privations, the young man reaches a settlement and discovers the instructor of his youth and his dearest friend,
an Englishman named Sarsefield. The story of Clithero,
previously related to Huntly, showed him to be a young
man of a peculiar cast of mind who was overwhelmed
with grief at misdemeanors, largely fancied, that he had
committed in England.

The former friends of Clithero, on account of in-
juries to whom he was now suffering remorse, now appear and Sarsefield is the husband of his former patron,
to whose niece he had been engaged. Clithero now disappears and when discovered is really a maniac, re-
garded with pity by his friends that had thought him
a double villain. Imprisoned as a lunatic, he escapes
while on board a vessel and drowns himself rather than
be recaptured. The mystery of the disappearance of
Waldegrave is cleared by the explanation that he is
slain by one of the party of Indians that had been com-
mitting depredations in the neighborhood.

The tale ends with all in contentment, but the destiny of Huntly, so far as marriage is concerned, is uncertain; whether he wedded Mary Waldegrave, the sister of the deceased, or Clarice, the former affianced of
Clithero,— this last on the common assumption of a
reader that such an one as Huntly must necessarily
marry one of the characters of the romance.

Prescott[1] in his essay on Brown points out that while the somnambulism of Huntly performs the same function as the ventriloquism of "Wieland," it has this merit over the latter in "that it does not necessarily impair the effect by perpetually suggesting a solution of mysteries and thus dispelling the illusion on whose existence the effect of the whole story mainly depends." But I think the difference is merely a difference in kind of method employed. Ventriloquism is suggestive of mystery and, if employed for deceit, its probable effects at once suggest themselves. Sleep-walking is not a mystery in its manifestations; hence, no mystery of the kind pictured in "Wieland" can be built upon it. I disagree with Prescott in that sleep-walking is manifestly used to explain several of the mysteries of the story, as the connection of Huntly with a band of Indians;[2] but, truly, as sleep-walking is thus of a different kind and also is not so prominent in the story, incidental rather than fundamental, it does not in the end detract from the strength of the plot as much, certainly, as does the ventriloquism of Brown's first romance. This, it seems to me, is the true distinction.

To bring two sleep-walkers into the story is surely a source of weakness. Apparently, Brown wants to bring Huntly into contact with the Indians without delay and the easiest way that occurs to him is to cause Huntly to turn somnambulist and reach the desired point unknown to himself.

1. Miscellanies C. B. Brown, p. 31.
2. Edgar Huntly, p. 215.

The story is in almost all places weak where the hero moves alone, for there, as in the case of Brown's leading characters, he is prone to "ruminate," to "meditate deeply," and to go over by himself step by step by a wonderfully slow process the incidents that have led him to his present position. The ability to grasp the situation and act upon it instantly is wholly wanting. Whenever anything approaching it is attempted the actor invariably makes a mistake, as when Huntly leaps from the precipice to avoid his supposed enemies. When Huntly,[1] after several wonderful escapes goes into a strange house and there finds Sarsefield,[2] his old friend whom he had not seen for years and who had supposed him dead, the older man, instead of considering it enough that he sees Huntly alive and before him, holds him at arm's length and with eyes fixed on the floor, goes over in detail in order to make sure of himself the unaccountable escapes through which he knows the young man has passed. Not only can the mind at such a time act no faster than the tongue can speak, but an escape from death is not satisfactory unless it can first be resolved into a syllogism.

The happenings that beset Huntly are such that we almost weary because of their seeming impossibility, but we certainly are prepared to accept more from him after being presented with the incomprehensible character of Clithero. No sane man would act the part of this character after he has unwittingly but most opportunely put Wiatte out of reach of inflicting more injury to his long-

1. P. 191.   2. P. 209.

suffering sister and to mankind in general. Again we have added proof that Brown, the philosophical mind analyst, did not comprehend the operations of the normal mind.

There is considerable power of description shown in telling of the wild scenery through which Huntly passed and the last half of the tale in particular is vivid and interesting, especially Huntly's escape from the first panther[1] and his encounters with the savages.[2]

Clithero becomes burdensome in the first part, but the author, as though aware of this, suddenly throws the hero into the midst of savages and thereafter there is interest.

It is the only one of the tales of Brown in which Indians appear and in the strongly drawn though brief illustrations of savage character, we at once think of Cooper, but there is no suggestion of Chingachgook and Uncas. The wildman of the American forest is crafty, cruel and ferocious, though no pains are taken to paint him in vivid colors.

When we have brought up Cooper, we, immediately, also compare Brown's description of forest scenes and, especially those in which savages take part, with like passages in Cooper. We note the absence of the free and easy swing of the narrative that marks the clear coloring of Cooper. Even in the most interesting and dramatic of the scenes of Brown, there seems always to linger a sternness and tenseness which fail to put us entirely at ease.

1. P 109.　2. Ps. 155 and 165.

Brown principally lacks movement, the passion for soliloquy in his principal characters being omnipresent. It is an analytical and so a philosophical trait, but when we are amid scenes where lives hang upon the issue of the moment, the soul demands a painter, a word-poet, not a mind analyst that stops to discover why we have thought and acted so as to draw ourselves into the present crisis. It is, indeed, because in this Cooper has satisfied us that we accord him greatness and to that degree to which we can ascribe this quality to Brown, we admire "Edgar Huntly." But Brown has but little of the genius of the prose-poet,—him that might write a perfect epic though he may not understand metrical verse. He is analytical, not expository.

Pride in his Americanism led to this—the first effort to lead the events of a work of fiction among savages and forest wilds. Hence, it is both interesting and praise-worthy, though it may lack artistic merit and contain many passages that are insipid and overcolored. In his preface the author says, "One merit the writer may at least claim; that of calling forth the passions and engaging the sympathy of the reader by means hitherto unemployed by preceding authors. Puerile superstition and exploded manners; Gothic castles and chimeras are the materials usually employed for this end. The incidents of Indian hostility and the perils of the western wilderness are far more suitable; and, for a native of America to overlook these, would admit of no apology."

CHAPTER VII.

CLARA HOWARD.

"Clara Howard" is a love story, pure and simple—exceedingly simple. The hero, Philip Stanley, is an orphan boy whose parents were poor. During the absence of an elderly benefactor, Howard, an Englishman, in his native country, Stanley becomes acquainted with the Wilmots, brother and sister. The sister, considerably older than Stanley, becomes engaged to him and on the death of her brother feels doubly her dependence upon Stanley, who has never known much of women. Mr. Howard returns accompanied by his wife, recently wedded, and her daughter, Clara Howard, whose father was a cousin of Howard. Stanley is taken into the family practically on the footing of a son. The young people become attached to one another but on his telling Clara of Mary Wilmot, she sends Stanley from her to fulfill his engagement, but Mary Wilmot has disappeared and the story dwells upon the details relating to this and to the restoration of Stanley to the favor of Miss Howard. Miss Wilmot finds consolation in another and all ends in contentment.

Experience in works of fiction did not add to Brown's ability in writing them, judging from the examples of the six taken for consideration. The story is carried on entirely by correspondence, for the most part between Stanley, Miss Howard and Miss Wilmot. This is a hazardous method at best as the author must, to make the story plain, cause the participants in the letter writing to say to one another many things already known by them, thus giving a stage effect to everything and causing us to consider that letter writing is the business of these people, not a means of social intercourse and improvement, or else that we have found people endeavoring to outdo one another in a mutual burlesque. In encountering this hazard, Brown has in no degree escaped the danger.

There is at the bottom almost nothing for a romance or even for a novel. A young man falls in love with a young lady while engaged to another. He neglects to speak of the situation until too late to be of use, but the second lady on learning of his engagement orders him to marry his first love with a dauntless self-sacrifice that reminds one of the parting injunction of the Spartan mother to her son going out to battle, "bring back your shield my son or be brought back upon it." The young man meekly strives to obey but cannot bring matters to a head as the second young lady knows she has lost his affection and she goes off to marry another, as it finally results, to the very great pleasure of the other two principal characters. We are constantly led to think that had the young people had less time from their business to write letters, there would have been less ground for a story and so they would not have made such fools of themselves.

Brown here falls into the sickly sentimentalism of the time as represented on this side of the Atlantic most prominently by Mrs. Tenney and Mrs. Rowson. I quote the opening paragraph, a part of a letter from Stanley to Miss Howard—a quotation typical of the entire story—"Why do I write? For whose use do I pass my time thus? There is no one living who cares a jot for me. There was a time when a throbbing heart, a trembling hand, and eager eyes were always prepared to read and ruminate on the scantiest and poorest scribble that dropped from my pen; but she has disappeared; the veil between us is like death." That the hero of a story could write such idiotic nonsense, and that to the one to whom his affections were given, simply because he could not find another to whom he had been engaged just when he wanted to see her, is enough to condemn the whole work.

The effort is to make Stanley the worthy, industrious, sensible young man striving to rise from poverty and obscurity and to create in Miss Howard a model young woman, but both are persons of moods and tenses, writing the most incoherent, nonsensical stuff to one another, alternately issuing and retracting stern decrees upon each other with all the solemnity of an edict from Rome. The young man has sisters practically dependent upon him, but he seems forgetful of his obligations. He is honest and upright, but mentions several times[1] how the wealth of Miss Howard strikes him most favorably, and this with more than the wonder of poverty. The actors suffer anguish of heart, but they never think of doing anything in such a case save to tell of

1. Ps. 329 and 330.

it in a manner that would drive to desperation the one
to whom it is told. Indeed, they seem to write letters
largely for the purpose of exciting one another or of
exercising their power to use a multitude of words when
they have nothing to say. Stanley, after receiving an
upbraiding letter from Miss Howard, gets wet and in-
curs a fever, which to his love-sick brain means certain death, and he immediately, out of fear that the
lady may not hear the details of his intrepidity, dictates
a long, carefully-worded letter to her, telling her how
he has gained his death saving another from drowning
and giving "the prayers of a dying man for thy felic-
ity."[1] Whereupon, as might be expected, the young
lady recants, the perishing hero survives and is restored
to his true love accompanied by much letter-writing
strongly punctuated with exclamation points. The tale
has not much to recommend it except its correct diction.

1. P. 310.

CHAPTER VIII.

JANE TALBOT.

The last work of fiction of Brown, "Jane Talbot," is the poorest of all. Jane Talbot is the daughter of a country gentleman whose wife has died leaving a son and daughter. The son is a worthless scamp, who apparently cares nothing for his sister and contrives to ruin his easy-going father by his wild and riotous extravagance. After leaving Philadelphia, the home of the family, he goes to France while the father dies, leaving the daughter to the care of Mrs. Fielder, a widow of fortune. Jane is prevailed upon to marry Talbot, a respectable, elderly man, who kindly goes off and dies just when the wife has become more attracted by a younger man, Henry Colden, of unsettled habits, who is exceedingly distasteful to Mrs. Fielder and the threat of disinheritance is held over Mrs. Talbot, if she does not immediately cast off Colden. After attempts at explanation and pacification, Colden, who has been maligned to Mrs. Fielder, goes away to a distant part of the earth where he is stranded on a savage coast and returns to America finally after four years' absence, weak from disease, to find that Mrs. Fielder is dead and Mrs. Talbot is still waiting for him, living with his married sister, so that the usual finale results.

The story, like "Clara Howard," is carried on entirely through correspondence and the same criticism

made upon that point in that story applies here, and
again it may be said that there is not much to recommend the tale aside from its good English; aside also, it
might be added, from its lessened use of ponderous
phrases as compared with the first four of Brown's ficti-
tious works.

The novel is full of gush and unhealthy sentiment.
The hero, Colden, is an irresolute young man who at
once "gives up the ship" when ordered to do so by Mrs.
Fielder and his demeanor toward her is but little less
than abject. Instead of minding his own business and
marrying the girl of his choice when both are ready,
after the fashion of the ordinary young American, he
bends the knee in submission, the world no longer holds
for him any attraction, he folds his tent and steals away
leaving the almost equally sentimental and insipid young
lady to mourn for years his recreancy. It is an illustration of what is true in all Brown's works of fiction that
it is indeed unfortunate for a young man if the romancer endeavors to make a hero of him. Colden is de-
ficient in moral courage and in the most important quali-
ties that give one success in life. Such an one has no
right to talk of those things entirely unfitted for him
for never could he provide for a family except through
outside assistance.

The unity of the work is considerably broken in
the first part by spending so much time upon Mrs.
Talbot's brother. Dowden, in his "Life of Shelley,[1]
quoted the criticism of Mary Shelley upon Jane Talbot:

1.   Vol. I', p. 473.

"Read Jane Talbot; very stupid book; some letters so-so; but the old woman in it is so abominable, the young woman so weak and the young man (the only sensible one in the whole) the author of course contrives to bring to idiotcy at the end." This criticism is of course dogmatic and uncompromising, but it contains more truth than fiction. Altogether, it would have been more creditable to Brown had some one else written "Jane Talbot."

CHAPTER IX.

INFLUENCE OF EUROPEAN WRITERS ON BROWN.

That Brown was affected in his works of fiction by his predecessors and his contemporaries in the art has been indicated, indeed, it goes without saying. Everyone is the product of his time and his environment. Now and then an intellect stands forth that seemingly has been able so to gather impressions from the "storied urns" of the past and from the realities of the present as to "send messages into Philistia" to appear like the warning voice of a prophet, or in other words of a man in advance of his time. The effect is caused by a higher point of view or by superior comprehension, possibly by both. The question then should not be,—Was Brown affected by other writers in his field?—but,—How was he affected by them? We must take it for granted that Brown, a "literary Doge," had read De Foe, Richardson, Fielding, Smollett, and Sterne. That he was acquainted with the lesser lights that followed admits of no doubt to one who has read his works. Had he not read most of those named at least, we surely could detect the fact, though we may not be able to say we see the positive influence of a particular author. The mighty movements following the French Revolution, when the works of Rousseau, of Voltaire, Montesquieu, D'Alembert and of Diderot came to invigorate all that read the English language, bore with full weight upon Brown as is evident from his first romance, "Wieland," and from his political essays.

It is stated[1] that Brown was an ardent admirer of Godwin and of his almost equally famous wife, who was an extremist on the question of women's rights and from her influence seems to have arisen his "Alcuin, a Dialogue on the Rights of Women." Dowden in his "Life of Shelley"[2] speaks of Brown as "Godwin's American disciple in romance." As Godwin and his wife were both ardent students of the French "Encyclopædists," we may say further that his literary friends must, in all probability, have lead him to the common fountain head. Both Godwin and Brown wrote much in the ruling spirit. Godwin was influenced by Utopian ideas and he believed, like his son-in-law, Shelley, that society should be overturned; hence his "Caleb Williams," the underlying principle of which is a character worked out by philosophical analysis to develop certain social and political phenomena in their effects upon the mind and upon society. It was using what we would to-day call the scientific method.

It is evident that Brown adopted this mode of presentation in "Wieland," "Ormond," "Arthur Mervyn," and in "Edgar Huntly." And in all his tales there is one character that stands out before the others with a second of nearly as great consequence. In dealing with these two characters in particular, and in an especial degree. with the former, Brown makes it his business to be

1. Pancoast Intro. to Am. Lit., p. 108.
2. Vol. I, p. 472.

careful in his developments of moods, to cause the changes of mind to come by gradations that we may see the effect psychologically and from it draw the les-. son. Sometimes he seeks to make the demonstration from other than the principal characters, as when with much circumlocution, he endeavored to draw the irrelevant and useless moral at the end of "Wieland." To point out the moral at the end of any tale is like telling a joke and then naming it, but in this we see some of the effects of his time which seemed to consider that we need not be expected to retain our common sense in reading or writing a novel or romance.

But in the first four of the works of fiction of Brown, and in "Wieland" in particular, there is an entirely evident attempt not merely to follow the manner of plot of Godwin, but to adopt his literary style. He endeavors by a few details, as in the description by Wieland of his crime, in the yellow fever scenes of Arthur Mervyn and in the escape from the first panther in Edgar Huntly, to impress the outlines upon the mind after the exceedingly simple but intensely sublime action of "Caleb Williams."

If Brown read French political and social philosophy, still more likely is it that he read Locke and Hume and was, we may conclude from his political essays, familiar also with the new science of Adam Smith and with the writings of Burke.

It is common to connect the name of Jane Austen (1775-1817) with that of Brown as though she in some way influenced him, especially through her best known work, "Pride and Prejudice," which exercised a very beneficial effect on the fiction of the time. But this novel was published in 1813, three years after the death of Brown, and all her works came forth after 1810. Accordingly, she could not have affected him and I fail to find any evidence of an influence from Brown upon her.

CHAPTER X.

INFLUENCE OF BROWN ON SHELLEY.

I at this point consider the oft' mentioned influence of Brown upon Shelley. Dowden[1] quoted the words of Peacock, that "Brown's four novels, Schiller's Robbers and Goethe's 'Faust,' were of all the works with which he was familiar those which took the deepest root in Shelley's mind and had the strongest influence in the formation of his character." But Shelley was only eighteen when Brown died and his wild, imaginative spirit was easily caught by the ruling sentiment of the fiction of the day which he attempted to represent and portray, but the "Romances of pseudo-passion and pseudo sublime" could not equal the almost blatant passion of "Zastrozzi" and "St. Irvyne the Rosicrusian." The former was written for the most part when Shelley was but seventeen. They are boyish creations and the influence of Brown can be seen only in the familiar predominence of the speculative and abnormal rather than in any one particular point of likeness. I have said Shelley attempted to portray the ruling spirit of romance but he could not do this without striving to outdo it. His nature would not admit of it. The boy gives rein to his imagination. Each character is intense. In "Zastrozzi" Matilda, Julia, the "Enchanting and con-

1. "Life of Shelley," Vol. I, p. 472.

genial female," Verrezi and the towering and haughty-passioned Zastrozzi are characters that appeal to us because of an indescribable touch everywhere of an artistic fancy. Undoubtedly Brown helped to give form to this fancy, but Shelley, even as a boy, soared above Brown, for his wild images could brook nothing ever builded by another. That Brown affected permanently the tenor of Shelley's writings I am unable to verify or credit.

CHAPTER XI.

INFLUENCE OF AMERICAN WRITERS ON BROWN.

Not so interesting because not so conclusive is the question of the influence of writers on this side of the Atlantic. In spite of the fact that during a part of his life speculative philosophy overshadowed Brown's religion, he was by nature deeply religious and highly moral. The intense and narrow as well as intensely narrow theological spirit of Puritan New England, the most cultivated part of America, added great stress to the conception that all writing should have a moral bearing, that nothing could be unmoral, but if not decidedly moral, everything must be immoral. Hence, the excellence of a tale was in its moral or religious strenuousness, and for that matter poetry and prose both were measured by the same cast iron standard. The horrible custom of constant self-inspection that reached its height under Hooker, the Mathers and Edwards had spent itself before the time of Brown. While the philosophy of Godwin led away from religion, Brown had the true Quaker spirit of his ancestors intensified by some lingerings of the creed of the author of the famous "Magnalia Christi Americana." Brown himself probably was unconscious of this last, yet one could not live in the culture of the north and escape it.

The great Unitarian movement had just started when Brown wrote. William Ellery Channing graduated from Harvard the same year "Wieland" appeared,

but James Freeman was re-ordained pastor of King's
Chapel in Boston in 1787 with a revised Non-Trinitar-
ian liturgy and the prenatal breathings of the work of
the Wares, Andrews Norton, Theodore Parker and
even of Emerson were in the air. Indeed, Brown was
active in anticipating this by his adoption of the philosophic principles of Godwin, which were really the
ideas of French and German thinkers modified by English minds. Moreover, the great transcendental movement meant nothing more than this; and Carlyle put
into English ritual the creed of the continent which
Emerson was to conform to American freedom and
vigor.

Whether Mrs. Rowson and Mrs. Tenney directly
affected him or not may be uncertain, as these ambitious
women simply caught the temper of English minor fiction in a more gushing style than usual, but it appears
to me that Brown seemed to consider that his first four
works of fiction were too intensely dramatic and dealt
too much with the impossible, so determined to make his
others more true to life. In other words, it amounted
to his dropping the philosophy of Godwin and coming
down to the same basis with "Charlotte Temple" and
"Female Quixotism," a basis made more enduring in his
case by his stronger hand and deeper common sense.
Brown could not drop his philosophy and write good
novels, but he might retain it and write good romances
for the time. The latter is what he did in his first four
works of fiction while his last two are merely novels a
few degrees better than the milk and water productions
of his two lady contemporaries.

CHAPTER XII.

GENERAL CRITICAL STUDY OF BROWN.

Brown's use of English is usually that of a scholar, but is what many would call over-scholarly. With him the study was not to find the simplest word or phrase to express the exact meaning but apparently to select the heaviest and most cumbersome. In "Ormond"[1] he says that clothing "stood in need of ablution;" again in the same[2] "all hope of happiness in this mutable and sublunary scene was fled." In Edgar Huntly[3] is stated "my stormy passions had subsided into a calm, portentious and awful;" again in the same[4] "the channel was encumbered with asperities." His characters never think or meditate, but it is their habit to "ruminate" so much that it becomes a pernicious custom. He invariably uses "somewhat" for something. One more passage will serve to illustrate fully his old-fashioned preciseness and insipid pedantry,—"Helena Cleves was endowed with every feminine and fascinating quality. Her features were modified by the most transient sentiments and were the seat of a softness at all times blushful and bewitching. All those graces of symmetry, smoothness and luster, which assembled in the imagination of the painter when he calls from the bosom of her natal deep the Paphian divinity blended their perfections in the shade, complexion and hair of this lady."[5]

1. P. 58. 2. P. 231. 3. P. 29. 4. P. 185.
5. Ormond, p. 116.

Brown had been trained a Quaker, but that in no
sense excuses him for his inaccurate uses of "thee,"
"thou," and "thine." They are introduced along with
the newer forms with apparent indiscriminateness. One
sentence uses the old, the next the new and soon
the old appears again with no apparent object for
the variation.[1] The kind of diction referred to is ex-
cessively common and in the eyes of the critic to-day is
far more serious than in the time of the author, serving
to render neutral many of the positive excellencies of
the work, as they are usually not merely faults of diction
but also of style. Undoubtedly, Brown might have im-
proved these things with better care. All the most important of his works were written within the space of
ten years and his rapidity approached that of Scott for
he was a very voluminous writer.

The close of our author's works is usually weak,
giving the appearance that he tired as he went on or
left them and became occupied in part by other things.
In "Arthur Mervyn" he apparently kept increasing
characters towards the close to compensate for actual
dramatic action. But Brown is not lacking in invention
or originality and we would never think of charging him
with plagiarism or with any undue imitation of another
author. He is conscientious everywhere and in everything. I agree with Prescott[2] that were his faults removed, he might not have been so good,—"*Si non erras-
set, fecerat ille minus.*"

1. "Edgar Huntly," ps. 135-136.
2. Miscellanies C. B. Brown, p. 53.

At any rate as he lost his Utopian ideas, his attachment for the theories of Godwin, as he came to be an ardent advocate of Christianity and endeavored to drop the extravagance of his first work, we may see in the religious experiences of Colden in "Jane Talbot," an effort to typify himself, but in making these changes he lost his power—the ability to describe graphically and to awaken interest in us by the almost indefinable something. As says Pattee,[1] "It is hard to lay down one of his romances unfinished; one reads on and on in a sort of ghastly dream until at length the end of the book completes the hideous nightmare."

Some men are great in themselves, others great in the eyes of the world through association with great names or because they mark epochs in events. Would Charles Brockden Brown be considered a writer of much prominence, were he not the first author of prose fiction in America? The day that would cherish writings with the style of Brown has passed. He did not possess the power, take him all in all, to entrench himself in principles of nature and of literature that are unchanging. He supplied the demands of the time with considerable credit and praise. A scholar with the instincts of a scholar, he did a scholarly work, but he had not enough individuality and keen discernment to discard the objectionable in contemporaneous literature and to write as the young prophet of the new and great America. A philosophic rather than a poetic spirit, he had not enough of the true and exact philosophy to un-

1.   Amer. Lit., p. 105.

derstand that to portray man in a form that will endure
he must be portrayed as he is and that nature to be
pictured so that the painting will be entitled to hang
upon the galleries among the works of great artists must
be tinted not in all the hues of the rainbow, unless it
has the rainbow's careful blending and that reality must
dominate art.

The spirit of the French renaissance united with
the culture of England and with the freedom of the new
nation was not sufficient to cause Brown to discard entirely the spirit of the old classical school of Pope,
while the so-called "nature movement" led on by
Thomson in "The Seasons" had been insufficient to turn
his mind to nature in her actual form. He could not
describe a cavern, a precipice or a deep ravine without
letting his imagination lead him into something that is
gruesome. Thus nature becomes not an emblem of the
bright and beautiful, but the representation of an infinite and awful power which hangs over and around all
things. This representation is expressive to us and we
should study it by night time when the stars are shining,
in the howl of the tempest when the sky is blackened by
storm clouds, but we should study it with a nameless, indefinable dread, we should "ruminate ominously" upon
it, go back to our "habitation" oppressed with melancholy and spend the night in a vague unrest with an
incomprehensible and indescribable something preying
upon our souls, to arise in the morning to new "rumina-
tions." And man is, though perhaps "The proper study
of mankind," yet a part of this terrible and mystic na-

ture, is always incomprehensible and the subject of
strange vagaries, whims and contrivances from on high.
We study these as phenomena of nature and, particularly,
as they relate to us and are "philosophical," but the more
we study, the farther removed are we from ourselves,
the more unfitted do we become to go on with the dull,
prosaic duties that devolve upon us. But we are to
"muse perpetually" upon it all, though never are we satisfied, never brightened, never go back with a glad and
cheerful heart to say,—I am of nature and of God. I
exist as a part of it and of Him. If he is great and
wonderful, aye, awful at times in his manifestations, I
rejoice in it, for it exalts me that see in it an expression
of myself. The Almighty is great and powerful, so am
I in a small degree as a manifestation in one form of
Him. Hence, I am glad to be alive, to see these mighty
movements all related to me and I to them. I breathe in
the air—an extraordinary manifestation of his power—
and it becomes a part of my being. I eat and thrive on
the infinite resources of a miraculous Providence and I
am a miracle. Therefore it is glorious to exist in such
greatness and, like Walter Scott, as a boy, to lie upon
the ground in a storm in the mountains and clap my
hands at each thunder peal.

But these optimistic feelings were not akin to the
soul of Brown. His philosophy was the philosophy of
darkness and distortion. He was too sickly and shall
I say too scholarly; not that he knew too much, for
scholarship and knowledge are not synonymous, but his
life was the morbid, introspective life of the study but

little influenced by the greater life outside. He read of
nature and of God from books but never fully realized
that he thus was getting these subjects only from a
meagre secondhand. The full, rich life of manhood, the
joy of living never touched him. He realized vaguely
that in the American Indian there is a creation different
from the ordinary and so something that we call "original" for treatment, but the thought became a fancy before it could be fairly comprehended. It slipped from
him ere he could write it down in vivid colors and he
remained sombre and desolate trying to write himself
into a great writer and philosophize himself into a great
philosopher, though he never yet had reached the life
he thought to describe save by fleeting moments and he
existed ever apart from what was and is in the highest
form the true, the beautiful and so the good.

But the fault lay not, I think, with himself, but
that he was by Nature so incomplete a representative of
man,—an illustration that he cannot be a grasper of a
number of great truths that is not well or vigorous in
organization. Brown had not the physical courage nor
the moral force to drop his books like Thoreau and lit-
erally to "take to the woods" for long months that he
might gain vigor and correct conceptions. He was
bound to his desk and only broke loose when necessity
drove him on brief excursions. Within the limits of
his strength, he did a great work. He realized his duty
to his country and to civilization to contribute as much
as within him lay and he never faltered though beset
constantly by weariness and disease. His patience, his

conscientiousness and his unfaltering devotion to the light that came to him led him ever on with a resolute heart and, even when disease was constantly preying upon him, his smile of affection always covered the deep-seated anguish. His pure and upright life was reflected in his writings, and if he could not write brilliant facts so that they would endure, all things of him exhibited the greatest of all truths that the highest virtue consists in "the perfection of one's self and the happiness of others."

It was then a courageous thing to be an American writer and especially to attempt to be the first American novelist, but Brown constantly displayed that courage. Had he not deserved to be first, the position would not have been accorded him. If he did not set the pace, he started the movement. It is with very great respect and considerable admiration that I have studied this "brief but blazing star" that during his short and sickly life worked with such unfailing earnestness along lines that to him seemed best and highest.

CHAPTER XIII.

INFLUENCE OF BROWN UPON AMERICAN LITERATURE.

But what has he done for us? That he was the head of an American school of fiction cannot be claimed. He lived in a transitional period in literature between the stilted, artificial style and what we are fond of denominating the "natural." Scott came soon after and prose fiction was recreated in him and never has lost his impress. Soon Brown and authors like him ceased to be read. Irving, not a romancer or a novelist, but a great prose writer, followed closely upon Brown. If Brown was the first American novelist, Irving was the first great American prose writer and his style tended to lessen further the influence of the first American novelist.

Cooper, the "American Scott," improperly so-called, ere long gave to American literature a right to look with pride upon its producers of prose fiction, and again a deep influence was exerted away from Brown. American novels that appeared soon after Brown were modeled for the most part after Scott and Cooper, as "The Buccaneers" (1827), S. B. Judah; "Rachel Dyer" (1828), John Neal; "The Betrothed of Wyoming" (1831) and "Meredith or the Mystery of the Meschanza" (1831). That Brown and others of his style will ever again be popular is exceeding improbable; we may almost say impossible.

Nevertheless, the influence of our author was considerable and valuable. Above the elements of weakness, we have shown, arose many elements of strength. The power of a great writer he had at times and we catch in "Edgar Huntly" shades of description and passages of strong expression that make us wonder if Cooper, though so different, may not have caught much that led him on from Brockden Brown. It is very probable. From the defects of another we see how to correct ourselves, and Cooper as he heard and read comments upon Brown could the better judge how he should act. Cooper, the painter of wild America and wild Americans is, indeed, different from Brown, the morbid mind analyst. Seemingly, then, only the touchstone of fancy could detect a derivation, but I am not one that think it necessary to be able to put the finger upon a point or principle of resemblance in one writer in order to be qualified to say with moral certainty he obtained assistance from another. It is too much to expect. We have in Brown a suggestion of Cooper. It is only a suggestion but it is enough.

For purposes of investigation and criticism, however, it amounts to but little to say that such an one, a writer, was a contemporary of another writer; therefore, the one influenced the other. We have the right to presume and assume that every man of letters reads the writings of other writers in his field and time and is affected by them, unconsciously perhaps and perhaps imperceptibly, but the influences are there and his debt to them is something; but I do not think that the spirit

of the Sunday School teacher that would read a moral
and religious lesson into every word of Scripture should
dominate literary criticism.   I am at times impatient at
the manifest attempt of many commentators to force
an issue where there is none and reason out an *a priori*
basis until *post hoc propter hoc* seems to be the law of
critical study.   Generally speaking, give a commentator
an analogy and he is sure to work out a derivation, but
the result is frequently as far-fetched and ludicrously
drawn as some of the various theories as to the origin
of the English manorial system.

Irving, who came next after Brown as a prose
writer, could take courage as the favorable expressions
upon the "New American" came to him, and I think I
detect in a few of Irving's works something in style,
though so different altogether, that reminds me of
Charles Brockden Brown.   The debt to Brown was
probably considerable of him who wrote to please and
in so doing to instruct, who believed in not taking life
too seriously or intensely,—a diametrical opposite of
Brown.

How far Brown gave suggestions to Hawthorne, it
is difficult to say.   It is common to reason thus: Brown
was a prose writer, morbid and sensitive, and so was
Hawthorne, hence the latter probably was something of
a disciple of his predecessor.   But in the first place
Hawthorne never to me seems morbid.   He liked especially to work out a peculiar phase in the human heart,
as the power of conscience in "The Scarlet Letter," but
that does not prove his morbidness.   We might as well

call every professor of psychology morbid because his subject is the human soul. Yet there is a very considerable likeness in conception and treatment between "The Scarlet Letter" and "Wieland" or between this and Godwin's "Caleb Williams." Hawthorne was not a renowned painter like Cooper whose fame rested in his bold vigorous strokes, yet he was a consummate artist who delighted in delicate touches, in the subtleties of his art; but Brown was nothing of this; still even in "The Marble Faun," I obtain a reminder of Brown. Here as usual we are unable to say one writer took his method of treatment absolutely from another. It might on as good grounds be asserted that Brown derived his manner of treating "Wieland" directly from Horace Walpole's "Castle of Otranto." However, if Hawthorne was not affected by Brown, he certainly was affected by Brown's mode of conception and unfolding of plot.

Again, we see in Brown a suggestion of Poe, the only distinctively morbid character in American literature, but if we think he suggests Poe, because Poe was morbid, we surely cannot discern much resemblance between the morbidness of "Wieland" and "Arthur "Mervyn" and that of "The Black Cat," and "The Pit and the Pendulum." But there is an actual sentiment in "Scarlet Letter" and "Marble Faun," one that never excites our ridicule whether we agree in it or not, while in the stories of Poe we observe great genius and great art, but the genius and the art of an intensely morbid nature taking the word morbid in its true sense of diseased. I cannot be sure that Brown conferred anything on Poe.

— It has been said,—and rightly I think,—that to study literature correctly and determine the value of the work of each author, he should be studied with reference to himself alone first, next with reference to his place in the history of the literature. Then, Charles Brockden Brown, not what is called a great man, yet deserves the place of first American novelist and romancer because he stood forth with enough of ability above the ruling style of such writings to confer to his productions that which we denominate genius, such that he was able to please and instruct his contemporaries, to dignify America by a new title and to serve in a respectable degree as a reference and an instructor for those that followed him in the hitherto untrodden field of American fiction

ERRATA.

(1) Page 20, instead of *Schuykill*, read *Schuylkill*.

(2) Page 21, instead of *alter*, read *altar*.

(3) Page 22, reference 4 is omitted with quotation from Prof. Beers.

(4) Page 35, in second line of second paragraph, read *is* instead of *was*.

(5) Page 65, in the fourth line, read *and* in place of *or*.

(6) Page 10, in the fourth line of the second paragraph, read *Calvinism* instead of *Calvanism*.

(7) Page 11, in the nineteenth line of the second paragraph, read *pleasure* instead of *fun*, and *spectators* instead of *audience*.

(8) Page 13, in the fifteenth line of the second paragraph, read *M. G. Lewis'* instead of *M. G. Louis's*, and in the following line read *Frankenstein* instead of *Frankestein*.

(9) Page 48, in the tenth line of the second paragraph, read *led* instead of *lead*.

(10) Page 55, in the ninth and tenth lines of the first paragraph, read *portentous* instead of *portentious*.

(11) Page 66, in the ninth line of the second paragraph, read *writers* instead of *writings*.

DATE DUE

NOV 0 5 2003			
GAYLORD			PRINTED IN U.S.A.